THE
RESURRECTION
AND YOU

THE
RESURRECTION
AND YOU

JOSH McDOWELL
and SEAN McDOWELL

BakerBooks

a division of Baker Publishing Group
Grand Rapids, Michigan

© 2017 by Josh McDowell Ministry

Published by Baker Books
a division of Baker Publishing Group
P.O. Box 6287, Grand Rapids, MI 49516-6287
www.bakerbooks.com

Printed in the United States of America

Library of Congress Cataloging-in-Publication Data is on file at the Library
of Congress, Washington, DC.

ISBN 978-0-8010-1954-8

Unless otherwise indicated, Scripture quotations are from the *Holy Bible,
New Living Translation,* copyright © 1996, 2004, 2015 by Tyndale House
Foundation. Used by permission of Tyndale House Publishers, Inc., Carol
Stream, Illinois 60188. All rights reserved.

Scripture quotations labeled ESV are from The Holy Bible, English Standard
Version® (ESV®), copyright © 2001 by Crossway, a publishing ministry of
Good News Publishers. Used by permission. All rights reserved. ESV Text
Edition: 2011

Scripture quotations labeled NASB are from the New American Standard
Bible®, copyright © 1960, 1962, 1963, 1968, 1971, 1972, 1973, 1975, 1977,
1995 by The Lockman Foundation. Used by permission. (www.Lockman.org)

Portions of this book are adapted from *Evidence
for the Resurrection* by Josh McDowell and Sean
McDowell, copyright © 2014 by Baker Books.

17 18 19 20 21 22 23

     7 6 5 4 3 2 1

green
press
INITIATIVE

Contents

A Personal Journey

What Happened When I Set Out to Disprove Christianity

JOSH McDOWELL

As a student at Kellogg College, I was preparing to go to law school and eventually into politics. Out of the entire student body there was one group of students whose lives were different, and they caught my attention. Rather than living for money, success, or fame, these students authentically loved each other. I came from a broken family, having been raped by our farmhand, Wayne Baily, every week for seven years. So I desperately wanted the kind of love they seemed to genuinely experience and display. Their love for all people, both inside and outside of their group, was weird to me. But I *desperately* wanted it.

But I was also an insecure skeptic with a big mouth. I didn't want them to know the hurt and pain that were deep in my heart. And I didn't want them to know how deeply I was seeking meaning and purpose in my life. Hoping to discover their secret, I befriended them. One day, as we sat around a table in the student union, I asked a girl in the group why she was so different from other students and professors on campus. I tried to pretend that it wasn't a big deal to me, but I *really* wanted to know. With a little smile, she looked back at me and said two words I never thought I would hear on campus as part of the answer. She simply said, "Jesus Christ."

Instantly I shot back, "Don't give me that garbage about religion. I'm fed up with religion, the church, and the Bible." This girl had a lot of conviction, because she shot right back at me, "Mister, I did not tell you religion. I told you the person of Jesus Christ." My intention was not to be rude, so I apologized for my outburst. But I thought Christians were losers and I was sick and tired of religion. How could someone who died two thousand years ago have any relevance for my life today?

To my surprise, the group challenged me to intellectually consider the claims of Christ. They actually dared me to examine the historical evidence for the Scriptures, the deity of Christ, and the resurrection of Jesus. I honestly thought it was a joke! And I was determined to prove them wrong. So I left college and, using money I had saved up from a successful painting business, traveled throughout the United States, England, and the Middle East to gather the evidence disproving Christianity. Today, much of this evidence can be found in books, at local libraries, and on the internet. But in the 1950s it could only be seen firsthand at libraries and universities around the world. I set out to make an intellectual joke of Christianity. What I discovered turned my life upside down.

Late one Friday afternoon, I was sitting alone in a library in London, England, weary after spending many months researching. Suddenly I heard something like a voice speak to me. I don't normally hear voices, so this was shocking and very unsettling. The voice said, *Josh, you don't have a leg to stand on*. I immediately suppressed it. After all, I was aiming to *dis*prove Christianity, not believe it. Interestingly, almost every single day after that, I heard the same voice, but louder, and louder, and louder! The more I examined the evidence, the more it took me to the opposite conclusion of what I aimed to reach.

My goal was to disprove Christianity, but my research led me to the conclusion that I could trust the Bible, that Jesus is God, and that he was raised from the dead on the third day.

Even though I knew it was all true, at first I resisted committing my life to following Jesus. I was afraid of what people would think of me and of the cost of becoming a believer. But now, after five decades of following Christ, I can wholeheartedly say that it was the best decision of my life. The evidence got my attention, but it was the love of God, which I saw on display in the lives of those college students at the start of my journey, that ultimately captured my heart.

The Resurrection and You is a book that my son, Sean, and I worked on together. If you are a believer, we hope that this will provide you with some evidence to see that your faith is well grounded. If you agree, would you consider sharing this book with a non-Christian friend?

If you are a skeptic, all we ask is that you read this with an open mind. If Jesus really rose from the dead, confirming that he is God (Rom. 1:4), then there is nothing more important in life than following him. If Jesus was not raised from the dead, then you have nothing to lose—it's all just a bad joke.

No one has changed the world more than Jesus Christ. And he is still in the business of changing lives today. Now, let's consider the evidence for the resurrection and what it means for *your* life.

1

Why the Resurrection Matters

The World's Only Hope

Consider this comment a girl posted on an atheist website:

> I'm confused . . . I always believed science would be the
> cure-all for my problems, but I don't know if I can keep
> living without eternal life. I guess I'll just have to find a
> way myself to make it through this meaningless existence.
> I just wish I knew of someone who could show me the
> path to eternal life. If science can't provide the answers,
> though, then who or what can!? *sigh* Doesn't it seem
> like there is a higher power that gives our lives purpose?
> Well, science says there isn't, so there isn't.[1]

Have you ever felt like this girl? Can you relate to her angst? Have you ever really wondered, in an atheistic universe, if there is any point at all? Even Bertrand Russell, the great and influential philosopher, realized that an atheistic universe is truly meaningless.[2]

Hope is in short supply in our culture these days. If life as one sees it now on this pain-filled planet is all there is, then existence is indeed meaningless and one must, as this girl says, "find a way myself." She realizes there is one thing that would make everything meaningful: *eternal life*. She once expected science to find a way for humans to live forever, but she has come to realize that it cannot.

At one point in history, there was a band of people who trusted in someone they fervently believed would truly change the world for good. A handful of devout Jewish people thought a man named Jesus was the Messiah— the deliverer who would break their oppressive bondage under the Romans and set up a permanent and truly godly kingdom on earth. Their prophet Isaiah had prophesied in the ancient Jewish writings that the Messiah would come and restore all things to a paradise, where there would be no more fighting, oppression, fear, or death (Isa. 11; 35). Everyone would live together in peace forever.

Imagine the terrible mental and emotional state of that small group of followers as they stood watching the Messiah, their deliverer, breathing his last agonized breath, hung to die as a common criminal on a Roman cross. They had given up everything to follow him. But now here he was, nailed up on a cross. Dying! And dying with him were all the hopes they had placed in him. They must have felt like the girl we quoted above. Life seemed meaningless. Everything was hopeless. There seemed to be no way out of their absurd existence, no pathway to an ideal, eternal life.

Mary Magdalene was one of those followers of Jesus the Messiah. She supported his ministry financially and believed he was the one whom God had chosen to bring eternal peace to the world. She stood near the cross and witnessed the cruel execution of her master, and now her life was in utter turmoil.

After the Roman soldiers determined that Jesus was dead, they took him down from the cross and gave his body to a wealthy Jewish official to be buried in a new tomb. Mary left the dismal scene determined to visit his tomb after the burial was completed. Early Sunday morning she went to the tomb, and there she experienced another setback. Not only had Jesus been unjustly killed but also, to her alarm, the tomb was open and his body was gone. Fearing that someone had stolen the body, she ran to Peter and John, two of Jesus' followers, telling them what she had seen. In utter disbelief, the two men quickly ran to the tomb to check out her story for themselves.

When they arrived, they saw the collapsed shell of the graveclothes still intact, but the body was nowhere to be found. Frightened and confused, the two disciples returned home. But Mary lingered behind. She peered back in the tomb for one last look, and what she saw startled her: two men, robed in bright white, sat inside the tomb.

"Why are you crying?" the angels asked her.

"Because they have taken away my Lord," she replied, "and I don't know where they have put him" (John 20:13).

Turning around, she then saw something even more remarkable: Jesus was standing right before her, alive! But strangely, rather than recognizing him, she mistook him for a gardener. Jesus asked her the same question the angels had asked:

"Dear woman, why are you crying?"

Still clueless as to whom she was speaking, she said softly, "Sir, if you have taken him away, tell me where you have put him, and I will go and get him" (v. 15).

But then in a moment of remarkable tenderness Jesus called her by name: "Mary!" he said.

"Teacher!" she cried as she suddenly recognized him (v. 16).

Jesus stood before Mary alive, healthy, and well because death could not hold the promised Messiah. God had resurrected him to fulfill his mission and bring eternal life to a sick and dying world.

Our Resurrection Hope

When Christ was on the cross, it seemed that all had been lost. Death had won. But after three days in a rich man's tomb, Jesus appeared alive again. The news was so shocking that his followers refused to believe it until he presented himself to them physically and invited them to see the nail marks in his hands and feet with their own eyes. Then Jesus made an amazing claim to his disciples: in the future they too would have resurrected bodies like his, bodies that would never deteriorate, age, or perish. They would realize the one great hope that would bring meaning to an otherwise meaningless existence. They would have new life without death or pain in the presence of a loving God forever.

That is the great hope Christianity offers to a hopeless world—an afterlife with God, free of pain and suffering, and filled with boundless joy. Despite what many critics claim, belief in the resurrection does not make us "no earthly good." In reality, it gives us hope for the future and impacts how we treat both people and creation in the present. This belief in eternal life is not a mere pie-in-the-sky idea designed to make us feel good in a hopeless world; it is a belief built on rock-solid evidence. We will explore the overwhelming evidence in this booklet.

The Vital Importance of the Resurrection

The historical fact of the resurrection is the very foundation of the Christian faith. It is not an optional article of faith—it is *the* faith! The resurrection of Jesus Christ and

Christianity stand or fall together. One cannot be true without the other. Belief in the truth of Christianity is not merely faith in faith—ours or someone else's—but rather faith in the risen Christ of history. Without the historical resurrection of Jesus, the Christian faith is a mere placebo. Without the literal, physical resurrection, we might as well forget God, church, and following moral rules. We might as well just "feast and drink, for tomorrow we die!" (1 Cor. 15:32).

On the other hand, if Christ has been raised from the dead, then he is alive at this very moment (1 Cor. 15:4), and we can know him personally. Our sins are forgiven (v. 3), and he has broken the power of death (v. 54). Furthermore, he promises that we too will be resurrected someday (v. 22). We can trust him because he is sovereign over the world (v. 27). He will give us ultimate victory (v. 57) and a meaningful life (v. 58).

British scholar N. T. Wright explains how central the resurrection has been in the life of the church:

> There is no form of early Christianity known to us—though there are some that have been invented by ingenious scholars—that does not affirm at its heart that after Jesus' shameful death God raised him to life again. Already by the time of Paul, our earliest written records, the resurrection of Jesus is not just a single detached article of faith. It is woven into the very structure of Christian life and thought.[3]

Although the resurrection of Jesus is much *more* than a historical fact, it is nothing *less* than one. We will show later that there is powerful, verified evidence that it really happened.

The Personal Meaning of the Resurrection

Freedom from the Fear of Death

It is common for humans to fear death. Not only is it extremely difficult to imagine ceasing to exist, it is also terrifying.

Why, exactly, do we fear death? Let us suggest six reasons:[4]

1. Death is mysterious and unknown.
2. We have to face death alone.
3. We are separated from our loved ones.
4. Our personal hopes and dreams will not be realized.
5. Death raises the possibility that we will be annihilated.
6. Death is unavoidable.

While the Bible never promises complete deliverance from the emotionally difficult aspects of death, we are told that victory over the utterly paralyzing fear of it is within our grasp. Truly understanding the biblical doctrine of the resurrection frees us from the debilitating fear of our final journey into the unknown realm.

The resurrection makes it clear that no matter how devastating our struggles, disappointments, and troubles are, they are only temporary. No matter what happens to you, no matter the depth of the tragedy or pain you face, no matter how death stalks you and your loved ones, the resurrection promises you a future of immeasurable good.

Fulfillment of Our Hopes and Desires

Science-fiction writer Isaac Asimov expressed the attitude many have about heaven when he wrote, "I don't believe in the afterlife, so I don't have to spend my whole life fearing hell, or fearing heaven even more. For whatever the tortures of hell, I think the boredom of heaven would be even worse."[5]

Sadly, a similar view of the afterlife is common even among Christians. Our vision of heaven is often limited to an extended, boring, uninspiring church service. Or many, influenced by cartoons and jokes, see it as a place where we will mosey about among clouds in long white gowns while strumming on harps. Somehow our image of heaven has become grotesquely distorted, and the prospect of life after death has not captured our imaginations or transformed our lives.

I (Sean) recently asked my students what they would do if they had only three days left to live before they died and went to heaven. How would they spend those few remaining days? Answers included skydiving, traveling, surfing, and (of course) having sex. I followed up with a simple question: "So, you think there may be pleasures and experiences in this life that if you don't do them before you die, you will miss out on altogether because they won't exist in heaven?" All but two students answered yes. The prospect of heaven dismayed and disappointed them.

Such a lack of eternal perspective sets people up for discouragement and sin. Many of them think that if they don't experience certain pleasures now, their chance will be gone and they never will experience them. They adopt this attitude because they carry in their minds a mistaken picture of what heaven is really like.

We have been taught too often to spiritualize the new heaven and the new earth with a nonphysical interpretation. Often when people call something spiritual, they mean it is nonphysical. This has caused a widespread misconception and has led to the idea that God's physical creation is somehow inferior to truly spiritual things, including heaven. Many also believe that in heaven we will be spiritual, which to them means that we will be without solid, substantial, truly physical bodies. This view leads to an unbiblical division between the physical and spiritual, causing many to think that only the spiritual is good and that the physical is temporary, disposable, and even in some ways evil.

There are serious problems with such a view. People who believe this way tend to forget that at the end of each day of the physical creation of the world, God pronounced his work to be good. Everything he made out of atoms and molecules, cells and dirt, he called "good." The new heaven and the new earth can't be merely spiritual (understood as nonphysical) because our physical bodies will be resurrected. A nonphysical resurrection is like a colorless rainbow. It's a contradiction! When the apostle Paul describes our own resurrection, he says,

> When the trumpet sounds, those who have died will be raised to live forever. And we who are living will also be transformed. For our dying bodies must be transformed into bodies that will never die; our mortal bodies must be transformed into immortal bodies. Then, when our dying bodies have been transformed into bodies that will never die, this Scripture will be fulfilled: "Death is swallowed up in victory." (1 Cor. 15:52–54)

Paul doesn't tell us here that we will be bodiless spirits. Indeed, he tells us the opposite. We will have bodies—real bodies like those we have right now, but they will be immortal. They will no longer be subject to the ravages of disease, age, and death, and they will never die. They will be absolutely perfect in every detail, stunningly beautiful, immensely strong, utterly healthy, and impervious to aging and death.

The world we live in now offers us a glimpse of the joys and pleasures that we will experience when God brings the new heaven and the new earth (Rev. 21). In his book *Heaven*, Randy Alcorn explains, "All our lives we've been dreaming of the New Earth. Whenever we see beauty in water, wind, flower, deer, man, woman, or child, we catch a glimpse of Heaven. Just like the Garden of Eden, the New Earth will be a place of sensory delight, breathtaking beauty, satisfying relationships, and personal joy."[6] We will not live in a sterile environment or float about among endless clouds with nothing to do. We will live on an all-new earth—just like this one, except free from storms, earthquakes, drought, floods, or any other disasters. Things will grow easily, and weeds and thorns will not exist. Animals will not harm us but rather look to us benevolently as their leaders and benefactors.

We may not be able to picture everything about our resurrected existence on the new earth, but this we can be absolutely sure of: God created us for delight. He created the earth for our delight and pleasure. Whereas all pleasures are now tainted by human rebellion, he intends none of them to be lost. All that was created will be restored. Because he loves us so deeply, he wants us to experience all the delights he originally intended when he created us.

2

Can We Know
the Resurrection Happened?

Is It True? Is It Believable?

Jesus' resurrection either happened or it didn't. It is objective reality, and so it cannot be true for one person and false for another.

How do we know this? I (Sean) once performed the following experiment with my students. I placed a jar of marbles in front of them and asked, "How many marbles are in the jar?" They responded with different guesses: 221, 168, and so on. Then after giving them the correct number of 188, I asked, "Which of you is closest to being right?" While they all agreed that 168 was the closest guess, they understood and agreed that the number of marbles was a matter of objective fact and not one determined by personal preference.

Then I passed out Starburst candies to each student and asked, "Which flavor is right?" As you might expect, they all felt this to be a nonsense question because each person had a preference that was right for himself or herself. "That is correct," I concluded. "The right flavor has to do with a person's preferences. It is a matter of subjective opinion or personal preference, not objective fact."

Then I asked, "Are religious claims objective facts, like the number of marbles in a jar, or are they only a matter of personal opinion, like one's candy preference?" Most students concluded that religious claims belonged in the category of candy preference. I then opened the door for us to discuss the objective claims of Christianity. I pointed out that Christianity is based on an objective historical fact—the resurrection of Jesus. I reminded them that while many people may reject the historical resurrection of Jesus, it is not the type of claim that can be "true for you, but not true for me." The tomb was either empty on the third day, or it was occupied—there is no middle ground. Before anyone can grasp the transforming power of the resurrection of Jesus, he or she must realize that it is a matter of objective fact, not of personal preference.

How does one go about finding a true answer to the question of whether Jesus did or didn't rise from the dead? A critical historian would check out the validity of the records of witnesses, confirm Jesus' death by crucifixion, go over the burial procedures, and confirm the reports of the empty tomb and Jesus being seen alive on the third day. Then it would be sensible to consider every possible alternate explanation of the event. Sound interesting? Hang on, because in the rest of this booklet, this is precisely what we will do.

Do Accounts of Miracles Undermine Credibility?

First, however, we must consider the possibility of miracles before we can openly examine the evidence for the resurrection. If miracles are impossible per se, then the resurrection could not have occurred, and we must look for some natural explanation of the events that seem to affirm it. But if we conclude that miracles are at least possible, then we can be open to following the evidence without bias.

As we make this study, we will do well to keep in mind two important considerations pointed out by New Testament scholar Dr. Craig Blomberg:

> There is an intuitive sense with which even the most devout believer must share the tension that the skeptic feels when it comes to the credibility of miracle stories. Moreover, even the person open to the possibility of miracles does not believe every strange tale of the supernatural.[1]

In other words, whenever we hear of an event that seems contrary to the common workings of the laws of nature, we naturally raise our guard. We don't want to be duped. So we compare what we have heard to the way nature works. And we know nature works according to established, predictable patterns.

Yet at the same time, we shouldn't prejudge the evidence by ruling out the possibility of miracles because they don't fit our categories. It is simply unscientific to determine the outcome of an investigation *before* examining the facts. To demonstrate the problem, consider the following true story. Near the end of the eighteenth century the Western world first encountered the duck-billed platypus. The platypus, which is indigenous to Australia, has fur over its entire body, is the size of a rabbit, and has webbed feet. Yet since it lays eggs, it reproduces like a reptile! When the skin of a platypus was first brought to Europe, it was greeted with complete amazement. Was it a mammal or a reptile? The platypus seemed so bizarre that—despite the physical evidence of the skin and the testimony of the witnesses—many Londoners dismissed it as a sham.

Not until a pregnant platypus was shot and brought to London for observers to see with their own eyes did people begin to believe. Until this happened, some of the greatest thinkers refused to accept the existence of the platypus, and others doubted the unique claims about its physiology. The problem, according to apologist Ross Clifford, was that "it did not fit some people's view of how the world operated, so they rejected it and they reached their verdict *even though the weight of the evidence said otherwise.*"[2]

The reaction of people to the story of the platypus is similar to the way many react to the resurrection. Many are unwilling to consider the evidence for the resurrection because such an event does not fit their view of the world. Of course, such a reaction reveals a failure of objectivity, allowing biases to overrule reason in considering evidence.

Rather than concluding before sufficient investigation that miracles are impossible—or even that miracles are certain to occur—we ought to assume a neutral ground that admits miracles may or may not occur. Then we can examine the evidence objectively and see where it leads us.

Craig Blomberg explains the position of those who defend the validity of both scientific law and the existence of miracles:

> Despite all the marvelous advances of physics, no one has yet proved, if God as traditionally conceived by Jews and Christians exists, why he might not occasionally suspend or transcend the otherwise fixed regularities of nature.... Physical science today seems to be much more open to the possibility of God than it has been for generations.[3]

Dr. Norman Geisler explains it in this way:

> Belief in miracles does not destroy the *integrity* of scientific methodology, only its *sovereignty*. It says in effect that science does not have sovereign claim to explain all events as natural, but only those that are regular, repeatable and/or predictable.[4]

Miracles are impossible only if it is assumed that God does not exist. Short of a demonstrative proof of atheism, one has to be open not only to the possibility that God has intervened directly in the world but also to the evidence that he has done so.

The Confirmation of History

The empty tomb, the linen cloth, the removal of the large stone, and the appearances of Jesus are either merely ideas in the mind or events in history. Hence, historical research is necessary to determine what truly happened that first Easter.

The evidence for Jesus' death and resurrection must be approached with an honest, fair, and open mind. Although we have our own preconceived notions and conclusions about the matter, we must not let the investigation be prejudiced by them. Let the evidence speak for itself. Historian Ronald Sider writes, "We have a right to demand good evidence for an alleged event which we have not experienced, but we dare not judge reality by our limited experience. And I would suggest that we have good evidence for the resurrection of Jesus of Nazareth."[5]

What we are establishing here is the historical reliability and accuracy of the Scriptures, not their inspiration. While the reader may come to the conclusion that the Scriptures are inspired, such a conclusion is not necessary to examine the life, death, and resurrection of Jesus as a historical event.

The resurrection of Christ must be examined by the same criteria used in examining any other event in history. The faith of the early church was founded on the experiences of people observing verifiable events in the real world. For example, Luke says,

> Inasmuch as many have undertaken to compile an account of the things accomplished among us, just as they were handed down to us by those who from the beginning were eyewitnesses . . . , it seemed fitting for me as well, having investigated everything carefully from the beginning, to write it out for you in consecutive order, . . . so that you may know the exact truth about the things you have been taught. (Luke 1:1–4 NASB)

Luke's careful intention was to relate actual historical facts.

Eyewitness Accounts

One reason for trusting the New Testament records of Christ is that they were written by eyewitnesses or from eyewitness accounts. Historian Dr. Louis Gottschalk, in writing about the examination of the accuracy of a source, says, "Ability to tell the truth rests in part upon the witness's nearness to the event. *Nearness* is here used in both a geographical and a chronological sense."[6] The New Testament writers were not passing on hearsay but events they personally investigated and, in many cases, saw with their own eyes:

- 2 Peter 1:16 says, "For we did not follow cleverly devised tales when we made known to you the power and coming of our Lord Jesus Christ, but *we were eyewitnesses* of His majesty" (NASB, emphasis added).

- 1 John 1:1 tells us, "We proclaim to you the one who existed from the beginning, whom we have heard and seen. We saw him with our own eyes and touched him with our own hands. He is the Word of life."

- Luke says, "He also presented Himself alive after His suffering, by many convincing proofs, appearing to them over a period of forty days" (Acts 1:3 NASB).

- Acts 2:32 reports Peter's testimony: "This Jesus God raised up again, to which *we are all witnesses*" (NASB, emphasis added).

- John says, "And he who has seen has testified, and his testimony is true; and he knows that he is telling the truth, so that you also may believe" (John 19:35 NASB).

In further support of their testimony, the apostles refused to renounce their belief in the resurrected Christ even though they were threatened, beaten, imprisoned, and some even killed for their faith. As the beginning chapters of Acts indicate, the apostles proclaimed the risen Jesus amid persecution. Because of their deep conviction that Jesus had risen from the grave, the apostles willingly put their own lives at risk. For instance, in Jerusalem the apostles were threatened and imprisoned by the religious leaders for their public proclamation of the resurrection. Nevertheless, Peter and John responded, "Whether it is right in the sight of God to listen to you rather than to God, you must judge, for we cannot but speak of what we have seen and heard" (Acts 4:19–20 ESV).

There is no record that any of the apostles recanted. And we know for sure that some of them were martyred.[7] While this alone doesn't prove the resurrection is true, it does show that the apostles really believed it. They weren't liars.[8]

Do Discrepancies Undermine Historical Reliability?

Probably the most popular objection to the trustworthiness of the resurrection narratives as found in the Gospels is the claim that they contradict one another and therefore are not reliable historical accounts. For example, the four Gospels tell us that Mary was the first to see the risen Jesus, whereas 1 Corinthians 15:5 says that the apostle Peter was the first witness. Mark says the women who went to the tomb to anoint Jesus "saw a young man clothed in a white robe sitting on the right side" (16:5), Matthew says an angel was there with a garment "as white as snow" (28:3), and

Luke says, "Two men suddenly appeared to them, clothed in dazzling robes" (24:4). Don't these accounts hopelessly contradict each other, thus destroying their credibility?

No. Statements may differ and not be contradictions. There may be explanations for the differences that do not undermine the truth of either. Therefore, the burden of proof is on the one who claims that a statement is irreconcilably contradictory.

While there are difficulties in the four Gospels, scholars should not be so quick to assume that they are genuine contradictions. Most scholars now agree that the genre of the Gospels is ancient Greco-Roman biography. This genre allowed the authors the same kind of flexibility in reporting that people typically employ in their daily conversations. Luke, for example, uses a technique called "telescoping," in which time is compressed to simplify the reporting of various stories. Specifically, he compresses the time of the resurrection, appearances of the risen Christ, and his ascension in a way that could leave the impression that all these events occurred on Easter Sunday. But John's Gospel shows that they occurred over a longer period of time. Is this a contradiction? No. Rather, Luke's compression was an accepted stylistic device in the genre of Greco-Roman biographies. To claim such differences as a contradiction reveals an ignorance of genre rather than calling into question the credibility of the Gospels.

The late New Testament scholar John Wenham, in his book *Easter Enigma*, offers a plausible harmonization of the resurrection events. After his careful investigation of the Gospel writings, he concludes:

> I had no real doubts that the gospel writers were honest and well informed people, . . . but I was by no means committed to the view that the accounts were correct in every detail. Indeed I was impressed in my early studies of the resurrection stories by the seemingly intractable nature of the discrepancies. . . .
>
> Reading all I could and studying the Greek text carefully, I gradually found many of the pieces of the jigsaw coming together. It now seems to me that these resurrection stories exhibit in a remarkable way the well-known characteristics of accurate and independent reporting, for superficially they show great disharmony, but on close examination the details gradually fall into place.[9]

Despite the differences, a closer analysis of the resurrection accounts reveals a hidden harmony. As philosopher Stephen Davis notes:

> Despite differences in details, the four evangelists agree to an amazing degree on what we might call the basic facts. All unite in proclaiming that *early on the first day of the week certain women, among them Mary Magdalene, went to the tomb; they found it empty; they met an angel or angels; and they were either told or else discovered that Jesus was alive.* There is also striking agreement between John and at least one of the Synoptics on each of these points: *the women informed Peter and/or other disciples of their discovery, Peter*

*went to the tomb and found it empty, the risen Jesus appeared
to the women, and he gave them instructions for the disciples.*[10]

Do Apparent Discrepancies Offer Positive Evidence?

Lawyers, philosophers, historians, journalists, and others have found that the apparent discrepancies, rather than diminishing the trustworthiness of the Gospels, actually support their reliability. N. T. Wright observes that the inexactness and breathless quality of the Gospel narratives actually add to their value. "This," he says, "is what eyewitness testimony looks and sounds like."[11]

Dr. Paul Maier concludes that "the variations in the resurrection narratives *tend to support, rather than undermine, their authenticity.* They demonstrate that there were several independent traditions stemming from some event that must indeed have happened to give rise to them."[12]

We will now look at some of the evidence that must be explained if we are going to understand what happened on that first Easter.

3

Evidence for the Resurrection

Was Jesus Dead, Buried, and Resurrected?

Christ's Crucifixion and Death

The Jews were well aware that Jesus had predicted his own resurrection. Fearing that his followers might take extraordinary measures to make it appear that Jesus had died and rose again, they took equally extraordinary precautions to be sure he was dead and remained dead. The first of these precautions was death by crucifixion. The death would be public, brutal, and certain.

The Brutality of Crucifixion

Crucifixion was a common method of execution during the time of Christ. Cicero called it "the most cruel and hideous of tortures" and the "extreme and ultimate penalty for a slave."[1] It was so gruesome and degrading that the Romans usually excluded Roman citizens and reserved it for slaves or rebels to discourage uprisings. It was used primarily in political cases.

"The pain was absolutely unbearable," observes Alexander Metherell, MD, PhD. "In fact, it was literally beyond words to describe; they had to invent a new word: *excruciating*. Literally, *excruciating* means 'out of the cross.' Think of that: they needed to create a new word, because there was nothing in the language that could describe the intense anguish caused during crucifixion."[2]

The Custom of Whipping

After the verdict of crucifixion had been pronounced by the court, it was customary to tie the accused to a post. The criminal was stripped of his clothes and then severely flogged by the soldiers. The Gospels record that Jesus was severely flogged before his crucifixion (John 19:1; Matt. 27:26; Mark 15:15).

The whip that was typically used had a sturdy handle to which were attached long leather thongs of varying lengths. Sharp, jagged pieces of bone and lead were woven into the thongs. An article in the *Journal of the American Medical Association* records:

As the Roman soldiers repeatedly struck the victim's back with full force, the iron balls would cause deep contusions, and the leather thongs and sheep bones would cut into the skin and subcutaneous tissues. Then, as the flogging continued, the lacerations would tear into the underlying skeletal muscles and produce quivering ribbons of bleeding flesh.[3]

Without medical attention these lacerations to the skin and muscle could kill a person within hours or a few days.

How Crucifixion Brings about Death

While hanging from the cross, it was very difficult for the victim to breathe. To inhale and exhale properly, he had to pull himself up by his hands and feet, which caused searing pain. In time the victim became so exhausted from the effort and from loss of blood that he could no longer perform the breathing motions, and he suffocated.

If the Romans wanted to hasten the victim's death, the usual method of terminating a crucifixion was breaking the leg bones with a club to prevent the victim from pushing upward in order to breathe. After the breaking of the victim's legs, death was imminent. The legs of the two thieves crucified with Christ were broken, but Christ's were not because the executioners observed that he was already dead.

The Spilling of Blood and Water

After Jesus was observed to be dead, one of the Roman executioners thrust a spear into his side, and "immediately blood and water flowed out" (John 19:34). British author Michael Green explains the significance of this:

> We are told on eyewitness authority that "blood and water" came out of the pierced side of Jesus (John 19:34–35). The eyewitness clearly attached great importance to this. Had Jesus been alive when the spear pierced His side, strong spouts of blood would have emerged with every heartbeat. Instead, the observer noticed a semi-solid dark red clot seeping out, distinct and separate from the accompanying watery serum. This is evidence of massive clotting of the blood in the main arteries, and is exceptionally strong medical proof of death. It is all the more impressive because the evangelist could not possibly have realized its significance to a pathologist. The "blood and water" from the spear-thrust is proof positive that Jesus was already dead.[4]

Pilate required certification of Christ's death before the body could be turned over to Joseph of Arimathea. He consented to the body's removal from the cross only after the centurion in charge of the execution had certified Jesus' death.

Jesus was definitely dead. The vast majority of historians do not doubt this fact at all. Dr. Gary Habermas points out that there is significant evidence for Jesus' death from non-Christian sources. These include Cornelius Tacitus (AD 55–120), who is considered by many to be the greatest ancient Roman historian; the Jewish scholar Josephus (AD 37–97);

and the Jewish Talmud (AD 70–200). Habermas says of these non-Christian writings: "Most frequently reported is Jesus' death, mentioned by twelve sources. Dated approximately 20 to 150 years after Jesus' death, these secular sources are quite early by the standards of ancient historiography."[5]

The fact that Jesus was actually killed is as certain as any event recorded in ancient history. We have to reject any theory that tries to explain the resurrection by saying that Jesus somehow survived his ordeal, appeared to his disciples as a bleeding wreck, and convinced them to tell people he had risen.

Christ's Burial

Many skeptics have focused on the events and environment surrounding the burial of Christ to find loopholes in the claim that he was resurrected from the dead. Therefore it is important that we look carefully at the historical facts and check out their accuracy and believability. As we mentioned earlier, the officials took several security precautions to prevent any story from arising that Jesus had come back from the dead. First, we will examine the facts about the tomb itself.

A Solid Rock Tomb

All four Gospels record that Jesus' body was placed in a tomb cut into a rock, and a large stone was rolled against the entrance. Matthew, Luke, and John state that it was a new and unused tomb (Matt. 27:60; Luke 23:53; John 19:41). Matthew points out that the tomb belonged to Joseph of Arimathea.

Archaeologists have discovered three types of rock tombs used during the time of Jesus. All were closed by covering the opening with a disk-shaped stone weighing an average of two tons. Each tomb had a groove, or trough, cut into the rock in front of it to act as a track for moving the stone. The trough was deepest immediately in front of the entrance and angled upward. The disk-shaped stone was placed in the higher part of the groove, and a block was placed beneath it to keep it from rolling. When the block was removed, the stone would easily roll down and lodge itself in front of the opening.

Clearly, if the body of Jesus was sealed in such a tomb, getting it out would take extraordinary effort.

We have key reasons for confidence in the burial of Jesus as presented in the Gospels. First, Paul confirms the burial story in 1 Corinthians 15:3–5. There is conclusive evidence that Paul drew from material predating his writing that can be traced to within three to eight years of Christ's death. Thus, the burial story can be traced back so close to the time of Christ's death that legendary development is virtually impossible.

Second, the tradition of the burial is not surrounded by adornment or embellishment. It is told in a simple and straightforward manner.

Third, no conflicting tradition about the burial story exists. There are no early documents that refute the burial story as presented in the Gospels.

Fourth, it is highly unlikely that Christians would invent a historical figure such as Joseph of Arimathea, a member of the court that condemned Jesus. Why would early Christians want to make a hero of a member of the very court that was responsible for Jesus's death? If the apostles were fabricating the burial story, they likely would not have invented a figure such as Joseph. The inclusion of Joseph as the one who buries Jesus in all four Gospels gives it the ring of authenticity.

New Testament scholar Raymond Brown concludes, "That Jesus was buried is historically certain. . . . That the burial was done by Joseph of Arimathea is very probable."[6]

Jewish Burial Procedures

The New Testament makes it very clear that the burial of Christ followed the customs of the Jews. Jesus was taken down from the cross and covered with a sheet. The Jews were strict about not allowing the body to remain all night upon the cross.

The New Testament tells us that two men, Nicodemus and Joseph of Arimathea, prepared Christ's body for burial (John 19:38–42). The Jewish custom was to place the body on a stone table in the burial chamber. The body first would be washed with warm water.

It was then the custom, as verified in the New Testament, to prepare the corpse with various types of aromatic spices. We estimate that seventy to one hundred pounds of spices were used for Christ's burial. This was a reasonable amount for a leader. For example, in the preparation of the body of Gamaliel, grandson of the distinguished Jewish scholar Hillel and a contemporary of Jesus, eighty-six pounds of spices were used. Josephus records that when King Herod died, carrying the spices required five hundred servants.[7]

The Use of Linen Cloth

After all the parts of the body were straightened, the corpse was clothed in grave vestments made of white linen. The grave linens were sewn together by women. No knots were permitted. No individual could be buried in fewer than three separate garments.

At this point, the aromatic spices, composed of fragments of an aromatic wood pounded into a dust known as aloes, were mixed with a gummy substance called myrrh. Starting at the feet, the body would be wrapped with linen cloth, with the spices mixed with the gummy myrrh placed between the folds. The preparers would wrap the torso to the armpits, put the arms down outside the wrapping, and then wrap to the neck. A separate cloth was wrapped around the head. The final encasement could weigh between 117 and 120 pounds.

John Chrysostom, in the fourth century AD, commented that the "myrrh used was a drug which adheres so closely to the body that the graveclothes could not easily be removed."[8]

Security Precautions

The Roman Security Guard

The Jewish officials panicked because thousands had been turning to Christ. To avoid a political problem, it was to the advantage of both the Romans and Jews to make sure Jesus was put away for good. So after the crucifixion, the chief priests and Pharisees said to Pilate:

> "Sir, we remember what that deceiver once said while he was still alive: 'After three days I will rise from the dead.' So we request that you seal the tomb until the third day. This will prevent his disciples from coming and stealing his body and then telling everyone he was raised from the dead! If that happens, we'll be worse off than we were at first."
>
> Pilate replied, "Take guards and secure it the best you can." So they sealed the tomb and posted guards to protect it. (Matt. 27:63–66)

The renowned Roman legions were the instrument by which Caesar retained custody of his vast empire. The Roman Empire owed its existence and continuance to these impeccably trained warriors, who were among the greatest fighting machines ever conceived.[9]

Many excellent resources attesting to the discipline of the Roman army tell us that a Roman guard unit was a four-to-sixteen-man security force. Each man was trained to protect six feet of ground. The sixteen men in a square of four on each side were supposed to protect thirty-six yards and hold it against an entire battalion.

Normally a unit charged with guarding an area would work in this way: four men were placed immediately in front of what they were to protect. The other twelve would sleep in a semicircle in front of them with their heads pointing in. To steal what these guards were protecting, thieves would first have to walk over the guards who were asleep. Every four hours, another unit of four guards was awakened, and those who had been awake took their turn to sleep. They would rotate this way around the clock.

The Roman Seal

Matthew records that "along with the guard they set a seal on the stone" (Matt. 27:66 NASB). Biblical scholar A. T. Robertson says the stone could be sealed only in the presence of the Roman guards who were left in charge.[10] The purpose of this procedure was to prevent anyone from tampering with the grave's contents.

After the guard inspected the tomb and rolled the stone in place, a cord was stretched across the rock and fastened at either end with sealing clay. Finally, the clay packs were stamped with the official signet of the Roman governor.

Because the seal was Roman, it verified that Christ's body was protected from vandals by nothing less than the power and authority of the Roman Empire. Anyone trying to move the stone would have broken the seal and thus incurred the wrath of Roman law and power.

Resurrection Facts to Be Reckoned With

Whatever one believes about Christ and his resurrection, everyone has to admit that something significant happened on that morning—something so dramatic that it completely changed eleven men's lives, enabling them to endure abuse, suffering, and in many cases even death. That something was an empty tomb—an empty tomb that a fifteen-minute walk from the center of Jerusalem would easily have confirmed or disproved!

Reports of the empty tomb and the resurrection appearances of Jesus Christ have shaken the foundations of thought and shaped the course of history from that time forward. Obviously something happened. Something big!

If you wish to rationalize away the events surrounding Christ's death and resurrection, you must deal with certain imponderables. The Jews and Romans took careful steps to make sure that Jesus was dead and remained in the grave. The fact that something happened in spite of their precautions—crucifixion, burial, sealing and guarding the tomb—makes it very difficult for critics to defend their position that Christ has not been raised from the dead.

Let's look at some of these events again and consider some conclusions.

Fact Number 1: The Roman Seal Is Broken

On Easter morning the seal that stood for the power and authority of the Roman Empire was broken. No one denies this fact. The consequences for breaking the seal were severe. When the person or people responsible were apprehended, they would receive severe punishment. Would Christ's disciples have dared to break that seal? Hardly! After his arrest they showed signs of confusion and fear. Peter even denied that he knew Christ.

Fact Number 2: The Tomb Is Empty

Another obvious fact that Sunday morning was the empty tomb. No one ever denied that the tomb was empty. It is significant that after the resurrection, the suddenly emboldened disciples of Christ did not go off to Athens or Rome to preach that he had been resurrected; they went right back to the city of Jerusalem where, if what they were claiming was false, their message would have been easily disproved. The resurrection claim could not have been maintained for a moment in Jerusalem if the tomb had not been empty. Paul Maier explains:

What happened in Jerusalem seven weeks after the first Easter could have taken place only if Jesus' body were somehow missing from Joseph's tomb, for otherwise the Temple establishment, in its imbroglio with the Apostles, would simply have aborted the movement by making a brief trip over to the sepulcher of Joseph of Arimathea and unveiling Exhibit A. They did not do this, because they knew the tomb was empty. Their official explanation for it—that the disciples had stolen the body—was an admission that the sepulcher was indeed vacant.[11]

Some have objected to the empty tomb story claiming that it was the development of legend or an apologetic device rather than a historical fact. But one of the most compelling evidences showing that the empty tomb story was neither an apologetic device nor a legend is the fact that it was first discovered to be empty by women. In first-century Palestine, women had a low status as citizens or legal witnesses. Except in rare circumstances, Jewish law precluded women from giving testimony in a court of law. Why would those who wanted to advance Christianity have contrived a legend that embarrassed the disciples—the essential proponents of the new faith—by having them flee during the crucifixion and instead have women courageously approaching the tomb and providing the first witness to its vacancy? Such a legend would not have served the purpose of advancing the cause. Common sense tells us that the best reason the women were reported as the first witnesses was because it was the truth.

Fact Number 3: The Roman Guard Goes AWOL

The Roman soldiers left their place of responsibility. This is a very odd fact that must be explained.

Dr. George Currie, who carefully studied the military discipline of the Romans, reports that the death penalty was required for various duty failures such as desertion, losing or disposing of one's arms, betraying plans to an enemy, refusing to protect an officer, and leaving the night watch.[12] To the above, one can add falling asleep (Matt. 28:13). If it was not apparent which soldier had failed in duty, then lots were drawn to see who would be punished with death for the guard unit's failure.

One way a guard was put to death was by being stripped of his clothes and then burned alive in a fire started with the garments. The history of Roman discipline and security testifies to the fact that if the tomb had not been empty the soldiers would never have left their position. Fear of the wrath of their superiors and the ensuing death penalty meant they paid close attention to the most minute details of their job.

Dr. Bill White, who was formerly in charge of the Garden Tomb in Jerusalem, has extensively studied the resurrection and subsequent events following the first Easter. White makes several critical observations about the Jewish authorities bribing the Roman guard (Matt. 28:11–14):

> If the stone were simply rolled to one side of the tomb, as would be necessary to enter it, then they might be justified in accusing the men of sleeping at their posts, and in punishing them severely. If the men protested that the earthquake broke the seal and that the stone rolled back under vibration, they would still be liable to punishment for behavior which might be labeled cowardice.
>
> But these possibilities do not meet the case. There was some undeniable evidence which made it impossible for the chief priests to bring any charge against the guard. The Jewish authorities must have visited the scene, examined the stone, and recognized its position as making it humanly impossible for their men to have permitted its removal. No twist of human ingenuity could provide an adequate answer or a scapegoat and so they were forced to bribe the guard and seek to hush things.[13]

Fact Number 4: The Graveclothes Tell a Tale

Even though there was no body in Christ's tomb on that Sunday morning, the tomb was not completely empty. It contained an amazing phenomenon. After visiting the tomb and seeing the stone rolled away, the women ran back and told the disciples. Then Peter and John took off running. John outran Peter and, upon arriving at the tomb, he did not enter. Instead, he leaned over and looked in and saw something so startling that he immediately believed that Christ had indeed risen from the dead.

He looked over to the place where the body of Jesus had lain. What he saw were empty graveclothes. That's all! He never did get over it.

The first thing that stuck in the minds of the disciples was not the empty tomb but rather the empty graveclothes. Michael Green has aptly observed, "No wonder they were convinced and awed. No grave robber would have been able to enact so remarkable a thing. Nor would it have entered his head. He would simply have taken the body, graveclothes and all."[14]

Fact Number 5: Christ's Appearances Are Confirmed

Few scholars today doubt that the disciples at least *believed* that they had seen the risen Jesus. Biblical scholar Reginald Fuller has boldly claimed that "within a few weeks after the crucifixion Jesus' disciples came to believe this is one of the indisputable facts of history."[15] What caused the disciples to have this belief? From the inception of the church it was claimed that Jesus appeared personally to his followers.

When studying an event in history, it is important to investigate whether enough people who were participants or eyewitnesses to the event were alive when the facts about the event were published. Greater numbers of witnesses help to validate the accuracy of the published report.

One of the earliest records of Christ's appearing after the resurrection is by Paul in 1 Corinthians 15:3–8:

> I passed on to you what was most important and what had also been passed on to me. Christ died for our sins, just as the Scriptures said. He was buried, and he was raised from the dead on the third day, just as the Scriptures said. He was seen by Peter and then by the Twelve. After that, he was seen by more than 500 of his followers at one time, most of whom are still alive, though some have died. Then he was seen by James and later by all the apostles. Last of all, as though I had been born at the wrong time, I also saw him.

Virtually all scholars agree that in these verses Paul records an ancient creed, or tradition, that dates before the writing of 1 Corinthians (mid-50s AD). In fact, many scholars who have investigated this creed date it to within three to eight years after Christ's crucifixion. It is believed that Paul received this creed when he visited Peter and James in Jerusalem three years after his conversion, which was one to four years after the crucifixion of Jesus (Gal. 1:18–19). This is why historian Hans von Campenhausen claims that this text "meets all the demands of historical reliability that could possibly be made of such a text."[16]

In these verses, Paul appeals to his audience's knowledge of the fact that Christ had been seen by more than five hundred people at one time. Paul reminds them that the majority of these people were still alive and could be questioned. This statement is as strong an evidence as anyone could hope to find for something that happened two thousand years ago.

Likewise, New Testament scholar C. H. Dodd has observed, "There can hardly be any purpose in mentioning the fact that most of the five hundred are still alive, unless Paul is saying, in effect, 'the witnesses are there to be questioned.'"[17]

The witnesses include some who were hostile to or unconvinced of his resurrection. No informed individual would regard Saul of Tarsus to have been a follower of Christ. He despised Christ and persecuted Christians, aiming to eradicate the entire Christian movement. Yet Saul, whose name was later changed to Paul, became one of the greatest propagators of the Christian movement in history. What could account for this radical transformation? Nothing short of a personal appearance by the risen Jesus could have sufficed (1 Cor. 9:1; Acts 22:4–21).

Consider James, the brother of Jesus. The Gospel record indicates that none of Jesus' brothers believed in him during his lifetime (John 7:5; Mark 3:21–35). In fact, they tried to fool Jesus into a death trap at a public feast in Jerusalem. Yet James later became a follower of his brother and joined the band of persecuted Christians, becoming a key leader in the church and one of its early martyrs, as attested by Josephus, Hegesippus, and Clement of Alexandria. What caused such a change in his attitude? Would it not be that James also saw Jesus after the resurrection?

Attempts to "Explain Away" the Resurrection

Many theories have been advanced attempting to show that the resurrection of Jesus Christ was a fraud. Since most of the facts surrounding the resurrection are undeniable, these attempts have relied on a different interpretation of these facts, seeking either a legendary, mythical, or naturalistic explanation. Few skeptics deny the essential events—the trial, the crucifixion, the burial, the guards, the seal, or the empty tomb—because the historical evidence supporting them is too strong. They simply deny that these events mean that a dead man came to life again. Their attitude can be summed up as, "Yes, but there's got to be some other explanation."

It takes more faith to believe some of these theories than to accept the explanation that is offered in the New Testament. We address each theory in detail in our book *Evidence for the Resurrection*. Here we will just say that a theory has to explain all the facts, including the fact that the apostles were all willing to suffer and die for their belief that Jesus physically resurrected on the third day. If the resurrection was a hoax, why would they willingly suffer and die for it? Some have proposed that they were under a mass hallucination, but psychologists tell us that hallucinations are individual experiences, and it is impossible for a group of people to have the same one. The alternate explanations just don't fit the facts.

4

What's Next?

How do you evaluate the historical evidence for the resurrection of Jesus Christ presented in this book? What is your decision about the documented fact of Christ's empty tomb? What do *you* think of Christ?

When I (Josh) was confronted with the overwhelming evidence for Christ's resurrection, I had to ask the logical question, "What difference does it make in my life whether or not I believe Christ died on the cross for my sins and rose again?"

In order for you or anyone else to answer this question, you must consider the words of Jesus spoken to his disciples: "I am the way, the truth, and the life. No one can come to the Father except through me" (John 14:6). The apostle Peter underscored his Master's bold statement when he said, "Jesus is the [Messiah]. . . . There is salvation in no one else, for there is no other name under heaven given among men by which we must be saved" (Acts 4:11–12 ESV).

Jesus claims to be the only means to a relationship with God the Father. The reason our relationship with God needs mending is because of sin. According to Romans 3:23, everyone—which includes *each one of us*—has fallen short of God's perfect moral standards. As a result, we are separated from a holy God and must bear the penalty of our own sin, which is eternal separation from God. Yet the amazing truth of the gospel is that we can have peace with God through repenting of our sin and expressing faith in Jesus Christ (Rom. 5:1). On the basis of the overwhelming evidence for Christ's resurrection and considering that Jesus offers forgiveness of sin and an eternal relationship with God, who would be so foolhardy as to reject him?

Christ is alive! He is living today! The most logical response to this reality is to trust Jesus Christ with your life and experience the personal transformation that only he can effect.

How You Can Respond to What Jesus Has Done for You

You can respond personally to what Jesus Christ has done for you through his death and resurrection through prayer. Prayer is simply talking with God. God knows your heart and is not as concerned with your words as he is with the attitude of your heart. If you have never trusted Christ, you can do so right now by praying the following prayer:

Lord Jesus, I need you. Thank you for dying on the cross for my sins. I open the door of my life and receive you as my Savior and Lord. Thank you for forgiving my sins and giving me eternal life. Take control of the throne of my life. Make me the kind of person you want me to be.

Does this prayer express the desire of your heart? If it does, pray this prayer right now and Christ will come into your life, as he promised.

Have you prayed to receive Christ into your life? Then, according to his promise in Revelation 3:20, where is Christ right now in relation to you? Christ said that he would come into your life. Would he mislead you? No! You can be sure that God has answered your prayer because he and his Word are trustworthy.

The Bible promises that by receiving Christ you have eternal life: "And this is what God has testified: He has given us eternal life, and this life is in his Son. Whoever has the Son has life; whoever does not have God's Son does not have life. I have written this to you who believe in the name of the Son of God, so that you may know you have eternal life" (1 John 5:11–13).

Thank God right now that Christ is in your life and that he will never leave you (Heb. 13:5). You can know on the basis of his promise that Christ lives in you and that you have eternal life from the very moment you invite him in. He will not deceive you.

How You Can Grow in Your Faith

You were not meant to live the Christian life alone. God's Word urges you to meet with other Christians to grow and remain strong (Heb. 10:25). Several logs burn brightly together; but put one aside on the cold hearth and the fire goes out. So it is with your relationship to other Christians. If you do not belong to a church, do not wait to be invited. Take the initiative. Call the pastor of a nearby church where Christ is honored and his Word is taught. Start this week and make plans to attend regularly.

If you have established a relationship with God through Christ as you were reading these pages, please write us and tell us about it.

Josh McDowell Ministry
2001 West Plano Parkway
Suite 2400
Plano, TX 75075

We would be delighted to send you some materials that will help you in your ongoing walk with God. You can also contact us through our respective websites: www.josh.org and www.seanmcdowell.org. At our sites you will find many helpful resources such as videos, articles, books, and other material to help you in your journey.

May this book and your decision to trust Christ make a significant difference in how you live as a result of your new relationship with Jesus.

Josh D. McDowell
Sean J. McDowell

Notes

Chapter 1 Why the Resurrection Matters

1. "SuperNinjette," message posted at www.atheistnetwork .com, July 16, 2007.

2. "All the labors of the ages, all the devotion, all the inspiration, all the noonday brightness of human genius are destined to extinction . . . that the whole temple of man's achievement must inevitably be buried. . . . Only within the scaffolding of these truths, only on the firm foundation of *unyielding despair*, can the soul's habitation henceforth be safely built." Bertrand Russell, *A Free Man's Worship* (n.p., 1903).

3. N. T. Wright, *The Challenge of Jesus* (Downers Grove, IL: InterVarsity Press, 1999), 126.

4. These points were developed in Stephen T. Davis, *Risen Indeed* (Grand Rapids: Eerdmans, 1993), 203–4.

5. Isaac Asimov as quoted in Randy Alcorn, *Heaven* (Carol Stream, IL: Tyndale, 2004), 393.

6. Alcorn, *Heaven*, 241.

Chapter 2 Can We Know the Resurrection Happened?

1. Craig Blomberg, *The Historical Reliability of the Gospels* (Downers Grove, IL: InterVarsity Press, 1987), 73.

2. Ross Clifford, *Leading Lawyers' Case for the Resurrection* (Edmonton, Alberta: Canadian Institute for Law, Theology & Public Policy, 1996), 104–5, emphasis added.

3. Blomberg, *Historical Reliability of the Gospels*, 75–76.

4. Norman L. Geisler, *Miracles and Modern Thought* (Grand Rapids: Zondervan, 1982), 58.

5. Ronald Sider, "A Case for Easter," *HIS* (April 1972), 27–31.

6. Louis Gottschalk, *Understanding History*, 2nd ed. (New York: Knopf, 1969), 150.

7. Sean McDowell, *The Fate of the Apostles* (Farnham, UK: Ashgate Press, 2015).

8. For more detail on the reliability of the New Testament manuscripts, see our book *Evidence That Demands A Verdict: Life-Changing Truth for a Skeptical World* (Grand Rapids: Baker Books, forthcoming Fall 2017).

9. John Wenham, *Easter Enigma* (Oxford, UK: Paternoster Press, 1984), 10–11. For another harmonization attempt, see *Jesus Christ: The Greatest Life Ever Lived*, comp. and trans. Johnston M. Cheney and Stanley Ellisen (Eugene, OR: Paradise Publishing, 1994), a revision of *The Life of Christ in Stereo* (Portland, OR: Western Baptist Seminary Press, 1969).

10. Stephen T. Davis, *Risen Indeed* (Grand Rapids: Eerdmans, 1993), 69, emphasis added.

11. N. T. Wright, "The Transformation of the Bodily Resurrection," in *The Meaning of Jesus: Two Visions*, Marcus Borg and N. T. Wright (New York: Harper San Francisco, 2000), 121–22.

12. Paul Maier, *In the Fullness of Time: A Historian Looks at Christmas, Easter, and the Early Church* (Grand Rapids: Kregel, 1998), 180, emphasis added.

Chapter 3 Evidence for the Resurrection

1. Cicero, *V in Verrem*.

2. Dr. Alexander Metherell was interviewed by Lee Strobel in *The Case for Christ* (Grand Rapids: Zondervan, 1998), 197–98.

3. William D. Edwards, Wesley J. Gabel, and Floyd E. Hosmer, "On the Physical Death of Jesus Christ," *Journal of the American Medical Association* 255, no. 11 (March 21, 1986).

4. Michael Green, *Man Alive!* (Downers Grove, IL: InterVarsity Press, 1968), 33.

5. Gary R. Habermas, "Why I Believe the New Testament Is Historically Reliable," in *Why I Am a Christian: Leading Thinkers Explain Why They Believe*, ed. Norman L. Geisler and Paul K. Hoffman (Grand Rapids: Baker Books, 2001), 150.

6. Raymond E. Brown, *The Death of the Messiah*, vol. 2 (New York: Doubleday, 1994), 1240.

7. Will Durant, *Caesar and Christ* (New York: Simon and Schuster, 1944), 572.

8. John Chrysostom, *Homilies of St. John* (repr., Grand Rapids: Eerdmans, 1969), 321.

9. The importance of the Roman army is underscored by Flavius Vegitius Renatus. A military historian, he lived several hundred years after the time of Christ. In *The Military Institutes of the Romans*, Vegitius describes the secret to the Roman army's success: "Victory in war does not depend entirely upon numbers or mere courage; only skill and discipline will insure it. We find that the Romans owed . . . the conquest of the world to no other cause than continual military training, exact observance of discipline in their camps and unwearied cultivation of the other arts of war."

10. Archibald Thomas Robertson, *Word Pictures in the New Testament*, 6 vols. (Nashville: Broadman Press, 1930), 1:238–39.

11. Paul Maier, "The Empty Tomb as History," *Christianity Today*, March 28, 1975, 5.

12. George Currie, "The Military Discipline of the Romans from the Founding of the City to the Close of the Republic," abstract of a thesis published under the auspices of the Graduate Council of Indiana University, 1928.

13. Bill White, *A Thing Incredible: A Reassessment of the Resurrection Narratives in Relation to Holy Week and Israel* (Israel: Yanetz Ltd., 1976).

14. Michael Green, *The Empty Cross of Jesus* (Downers Grove, IL: InterVarsity Press, 1984), 22–23.

15. Reginald H. Fuller, *The Foundations of New Testament Christology* (New York: Scribner's, 1965), 142.

16. Hans von Campenhausen, "The Events of Easter and the Empty Tomb," in *Tradition and Life in the Early Church* (Philadelphia: Fortress, 1968), 44.

17. C. H. Dodd, "The Appearances of the Risen Christ: A Study in Form-Criticism of the Gospels," in *More New Testament Studies* (Manchester, UK: University of Manchester Press, 1968), 128.

ALSO BY BESTSELLING AUTHORS
JOSH McDOWELL AND SEAN McDOWELL

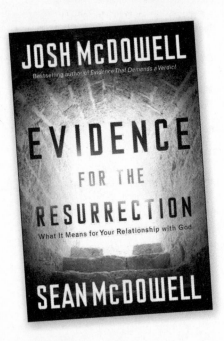

In this fascinating look at the claims of the Gospel writers and two thousand years of believing Christians, bestselling authors Josh McDowell and his son, Sean, examine the compelling evidence and conclude that Jesus Christ conquered death and the grave.

Learn more about
JOSH McDOWELL
MINISTRY

f @JMMinistry

🐦 @Josh_McDowell

▶ JoshMcDowell

📷 JoshDMcDowell

📌 JoshMcDowell

www.Josh.org/Blog